THE PSYCHONAUT'S GUIDEBOOK

A Field Guide to a Good Trip

Wherever and whenever humans have lived
they have gathered together to get intoxicated.

The world experienced in sober solitude is not,
and never has been, quite enough.

The drugs vary of course,
but they are always there.

- Mark Forsyth,
A Short History of Drunkenness

INTRODUCTION

I wrote this book to provide context and guidance for people with little or no experience with psychedelic drugs. This should help anyone who has never tripped understand what a psychedelic trip is all about. If you are curious about tripping, are trying to decide if you want to trip, or are actively planning one of your first trips, you should find this useful.

This book is designed for the self-guided tripper. While any psychedelic trip has the capacity to be therapeutic or spiritual, this book is not meant to guide you at that level. If you are looking to psychedelics to treat an existing condition such as addiction, depression, anxiety, or a crisis of faith, I recommend that you seek out the services of a trained guide.

If you are a new explorer looking to experience the powerful landscape of the psychedelic trip, this book is for you. It will provide a map to the world of adventure inside your own mind.

Becoming educated about the psychedelic experience is like sex ed—being informed can save you from a lot of unnecessary grief. The drive to discover altered states of consciousness is as powerful in some of us as the drive to have sex. And like sex, preaching abstinence doesn't prevent people from doing it, it just prevents them from being safe. I believe that education about altered consciousness should be available to anyone who is interested.

Due to the unfortunate legal status of these substances, my qualifications to draw this map for you are not a series of letters after my name on the cover of this book. Instead, they come from my experience as a psychonaut (an explorer of psychedelic experiences) and as a guide for other psychonauts.

I took my first psychedelic trip on mushrooms in the spring of 1994. As a teenager ravenous for adventure, I was utterly fascinated. I marveled at the depth of the music playing from a cassette ("Rift" by Phish), and I worshiped the moon with the entirety of my being (until she asked me to stop). Entranced by this new experience, I began to trip about once a month, sometimes more, for the next several years.

I started tripping right when the world wide web first went public, so there wasn't very much information widely available yet on substances that had been outlawed. What I did find was a subculture that had been quietly existing since the sixties. Hippies were giving way to ravers, and psychedelic use was generally seen as purely recreational. In that environment, I was fortunate to stumble across a community of psychonauts that had read some of the mind-bending literature of the early 60s and who wanted to find out if the psychedelic experience could be useful for more than just a good time.

Some of them built a discussion group that included a mailing list and an Internet Relay Chat (IRC) channel. While we discussed the psychedelic experience, we became a community. We experimented in groups small and large, holding an annual in-person event that often had over a hundred attendees. We tapped into advice from our elders who had experienced tripping in the sixties and seventies, and actively discussed ideas on how to adjust our experiences for maximum fun and benefit.

I spent twelve years regularly tripping, and I viewed each trip as research. My goal was to understand what psychedelics do, how that can be leveraged for personal development, and how to build an optimum environment to facilitate that experience. Six years in, I began to host three-day long retreats for up to fifty trippers.

Eventually, I left the psychedelic community to settle down with a family. I could not continue to do work that was criminalized while being responsible for the people that I brought into this world.

My children are now becoming teenagers and I've realized how important it is to pass on what I've learned to the next generation. In addition, friends of my generation have begun asking for my advice as they discover psychedelics in mid-life. This pocket guide to the psychedelic experience will help you understand what psychedelics are and what they are good for. It will give you an overview of the space psychedelics create and teach you to build the optimum environment in which to navigate that space. It will help you stay safe on your adventure and understand what happened in it. Like any good guidebook, it will enhance your trip.

Context

Humans are not a sober species. From prehistoric times to modern day, humans have been driven to alter our consciousness. Depending on local availability, people have used nicotine, caffeine, alcohol, cannabinoids, opiates, and psychedelics for longer than we have kept a recorded history. We have archeological evidence of residual amounts of psychoactive compounds on artifacts that were probably tools for getting high. While not all ancient cultures were using psychedelics, it is clear that to trip is human.

Psilocybin mushrooms can be found across the globe in all temperate regions. Symbols of mushrooms are found on Meso-American artifacts, as well as shapes of the psilocybin-bearing fruits of the local plants and flowers. The same can be said of the mescaline-producing peyote cactus found in the American Southwest and parts of Mexico. Ancient Greeks used a psychedelic cousin to LSD in a drink called kykeon during the sacred rites of the Eleusinian Mysteries. Laplanders are known to have consumed the urine of reindeer who grazed on psychedelic lichen. The Nepalese sometimes eat "mad honey," harvested from bees that feed on the nectar of certain native rhododendrons that contain hallucinogenic compounds. There are a multitude of ways that people have tripped around the world and throughout history, but their experiences have most often been contained within a cultural context that doesn't exist in modern western culture.

Alcohol has long been the dominant intoxicant in Western cultures. We have traditions around drinking alcohol that are mostly social, including during meals, making toasts, pairing wines with food, and we also use it for religious purposes such as the wine in the Christian sacrament. But we don't have traditions surrounding psychedelic use. That is why it is so important to learn about psychedelics and how they will affect you. You weren't raised with a cultural understanding as you were with alcohol, and most of the stories our culture tells us about psychedelics are misleading at best.

The cultural revolution of the 1960's brought with it the invention of LSD (lycergic acid diethylamide, a drug derived from a fungus) and the re-discovery of psilocybin mushrooms to the modern world. Timothy Leary told us to "Turn on, tune in, and drop out." The music of the era

sang to us about the wonders of psychedelic
drug use. A movement toward peace, equality,
and environmentalism grew. Along with it grew
political and puritanical opposition.

In 1970, the Controlled Substances Act began
the era of psychedelic prohibition. In 1971, Nixon declared the War on Drugs. In 1994 it was
made public that Nixon had created the War
on Drugs to bolster his political base by criminalizing "the antiwar left, and black people."
President Nixon's domestic policy chief, John
Ehrlichman, was quoted as saying: "We knew
we couldn't make it illegal to be either against
the war or black, but by getting the public to
associate the hippies with marijuana and blacks
with heroin, and then criminalizing both heavily,
we could disrupt those communities. We could
arrest their leaders, raid their homes, break up
their meetings, and vilify them night after night
on the evening news. Did we know we were
lying about the drugs? Of course we did." (in an
interview with Dan Baum for his book Smoke
and Mirrors: The War on Drugs and the Politics
of Failure c. 1996) While this quote may be an
exaggeration of the events 25 years earlier, it is
clear that prohibition was political and targeted
at specific groups of Americans. In 1986, Ronald
Reagan's Anti-Drug Abuse Act intensified this

effect by increasing penalties and instigating mass incarceration of minorities.

Psychedelics (and other drugs, including marijuana) were made illegal not just because they pose a potential danger to the individual, but also because they were dangerous to a power structure.

The War on Drugs is receding, but it has left a strong mark on more than just American culture. It has led to black and white thinking about psychedelics, which can be detrimental to safe usage. Thinking that psychedelics are dangerous because they are illegal takes away the opportunity to understand psychedelic use and its possible benefits. Psychedelics are not drugs of abuse. They can be abused, but they are not inherently addictive or damaging. Quite the opposite. On the other hand, thinking that psychedelics are perfectly safe because they were made illegal under false pretenses can lead to a cavalier approach to a powerful substance that deserves awareness and respect. Awareness of our biases help us see more clearly. Such value judgments can only cloud understanding.

Altering our consciousness can provide personal and cultural insights. Those insights can help us to become the best versions of ourselves by

providing a path to meaning, beauty, and understanding. Altering our consciousness is a risk,
but one that can be mitigated through responsible behavior.

Set, Setting, and Substance

There are three forces that shape the psychedelic experience: set, setting, and substance. Set refers to your mindset. Setting describes your environment. Substance is what you have ingested, and how much. Together, these three build the framework of your experience.

Set

To understand your mindset, you must understand yourself and your motivations. This will help you decide whether taking a psychedelic is right for you at this time.

What are some good reasons to take psychedelics? Are you driven by a desire for an adventure? Are you curious about what it is like? Are you looking to learn more about yourself? Are you looking for a tool to facilitate your quest to be the best version of yourself? Are you seeking an experience of the numinous? All of these are valid reasons to enter the psychedelic space.

Psychedelics alter our perceptions of the ordinary, creating a metamorphosis that transforms a social gathering into an epic adventure. The experience opens new avenues for conversation, imagination, and interaction. Habits and assumptions are up for question. Simple actions become challenging as you experience each step with fresh awareness. Art gains new dimensions as you become aware of aspects you never noticed, while your mind creates its own resonant content. It is called tripping because it is so much like taking a trip to somewhere new.

Sometimes we travel to a new place just to see it, experience it, discover it. Sometimes we travel to a new place to find ourselves outside of our comforts and routines. Tripping is very useful for this goal as well. Psychedelics can let us shed the patterns of our life from the comfort of our own homes, allowing us the mental space to learn about ourselves. This is facilitated by an induced mental plasticity that encourages your thoughts to move freely from their well-trodden pathways. This creates a mental environment where you can find new ways to think that are more useful for you.

Another reason that we travel is to go on a

pilgrimage. Given the appropriate circumstances, the psychedelic space can provide access to a spiritual realm. What that place is and what it means remains a mystery. What we do know is that those who go there usually return with a sense of connection to all life and being at peace with the universe.

To extend the travel metaphor, there are also several trip advisories. Just as there are good reasons to try them, there are good reasons to avoid them, unless you have a trained professional to guide you. If you have recently experienced a trauma or you are very preoccupied with a negative situation in your life, tripping could act like ripping off a bandage before a wound has properly healed. Such experiences are unpleasant and counterproductive.

If you have a severe mental health disability, do not trip without the guidance of a trained professional. Psychedelics create a mental plasticity that can be a very useful tool for improving mental health, but that plasticity can also lower any mental scaffolding that you may be using to keep yourself functional. If you are using any mental crutches to stabilize yourself as you care for your mental illness, do not trip.

There is some evidence that psychoactive drugs

such as cannabis, LSD, cocaine, and amphetamines can trigger schizophrenia or similar illnesses. If you have a genetic disposition to schizophrenia or other psychotic disorders, research your risk factors before taking psychoactives. Not all psychoactive drugs are psychedelic, so don't assume a drug is psychologically safe just because it isn't technically a psychedelic.

Some medications are contraindicated with the use of psychedelics. For example, MAOIs (such as selegiline, isocarboxazid, phenelzine, and tranylcypromine) may increase the effects of psychedelics while SSRIs (such as fluoxetine, citalopram, escitalopram, paroxetine, and sertraline) and antipsychotics (Latuda, Abilify, Thorazine) may prevent the psychedelic from taking effect, depending on which psychedelic drug they are interacting with. Lithium, tricyclics, ritonavir, or indinavir may cause dangerous interactions. Psychedelics are drugs, and as with any drug, check their interactions with the other drugs that may be in your system.

Most importantly, do not take a psychedelic if you do not want to. Trust your gut and don't capitulate to any external pressures to take psychedelics. Your decision to go on a psychedelic trip can only come from you.

The greatest trips are the ones where you bring mindful intention while allowing space for the unexpected. The act of bringing intention to a psychedelic experience is called metaprogramming. This term now refers to a computer that can program itself, but in a psychedelic context, our own minds are the computer. Cognitive Behavior Therapy (CBT) takes a similar approach, using talk therapy to move oneself away from negative behaviors. Metaprogramming with psychedelics uses mindful intention to leverage the malleability of the psychedelic mind-state to encourage yourself to focus on the positive aspects of the human experience.

Imagine your mind is like a forest, and the trees are made out of the reality that you experience every day. You maneuver around those trees with thoughts. These thoughts create pathways in your mind. Every time we think a thought, we tread that path and make it more likely that we will think that way again in the future. Psychedelics create a plasticity in the forest of your mind by temporarily diminishing all of the underbrush. This gives you the opportunity to reroute your mental paths with intention.

Some common intentions for metaprogramming include increased awareness of one's own emotions, learning to live in the moment, increasing one's openness to new ideas, bringing awareness to assumptions, observing without judgment, building a better narrative, evaluating priorities, connecting with existence, and experiencing awe. These intentions can be specific or broad, but it is useful to enter your experience with an intention. This is a key aspect of influencing your mindset. To solidify these intentions, it may be useful to write them down or share them with your companions at the beginning of your trip.

Psychedelics exhibit a strong expectancy effect. You are likely to experience what you expect to experience. Use this to your benefit. Even if your entire purpose is just to see what tripping is all about, choose an intention for your trip such as "connect with existence" or "experience awe" as a way to set yourself up for a positive experience. If you are looking to explore a more specific goal, keep it positive. Frame your goal in terms of the good thing you are moving toward, such as "discover what is most important to me" or "improve the tone of my internal dialog." These intentions will guide you to a positive experience, which is particularly important for your first trips.

Whichever intention you decide to pursue, look at it from as many sides as possible in the day or two leading up to your trip. When you find yourself anticipating your upcoming trip, use that mental energy to inspect your intention. The better you understand your intention while sober, the more ground you are likely to be able to cover while tripping. Taking time before a trip for meditation can similarly improve your experience. Psychedelics provide a heightened sense of mindfulness which can be amplified by preparing for a trip with a mindfulness practice.

Be curious about where your trip will take you. While it is important to approach your trip with intention, do not try to forcefully impose your intention upon your trip. Do not demand that your trip take you where you want to go. Ask your trip to lead you to your goal. Your path may not be direct or what you expected, so accept deviations from your intention as gifts from your subconscious. More often than not, they will be amazing.

What if your trip takes you somewhere dark? There is an old maxim: "There are no bad trips, only difficult ones." In the overwhelming majority of challenging trips, the solution is to confront the darkness. Running away from a useful (albeit daunting) experience heightens the difficulty in dealing with it. Face whatever is bothering you and ask what the experience needs you to understand. Do not fear a challenging trip. Facing your anxiety can lead to the greatest moments of self-discovery and be a precursor to the greatest moments of bliss.

Setting

The second force that structures your psychedelic experience is the setting. This refers to the location in which you will trip and the people with whom you will be tripping. Where should you take psychedelics? Who should you take them with? Should you stay at home or go out? In private or public? In a setting that is urban or rural? The answer to each of these questions will shape your experience, and there are key considerations for each possibility.

Early experiences should be in a comfortable private space accompanied by people with whom you feel safe. You may not realize how many masks you wear when you interact with public spaces and strangers, but a psychedelic will remove many (and possibly all) of your masks. Choose an environment where you do not need them as your experience will hinge on how safe you feel. At minimum, you will need one other person as a companion. Often that means a friend to trip with, but sometimes it means Ground Control.

Ground Control is the psychedelic version of a designated driver or babysitter. Having Ground Control is recommended in situations where there is a solo tripper, an excursion to a public space, or any trip where it feels like the right thing to do. Like a designated driver, Ground Control can be particularly useful if you need to get home after a trip at a festival or museum. Navigating rideshare or public transportation while on a psychedelic is like navigating rideshare or public transportation while drunk in a foreign country. You can do it, but it sounds way more interesting than it actually is. Let Ground Control drive the car, use the app, or buy the tickets.

Ground Control is useful in any situation where you need someone tethered to consensual reality. Venturing out into public is the most common use for Ground Control, but they are also very useful for large groups of trippers or solo trippers. In large groups of trippers, situations are more likely to arise where it is useful to have a sober person. When tripping solo, Ground Control acts as a buffer so that the tripper can focus on their experience instead of the environment.

If you are attending a festival and will be around a very large group of people, curate a small, two to four person group that will stay together for the entire experience. If you are tripping with a private group, make sure that you feel comfortable around everyone there. If you wouldn't go on a road trip with these people, you probably shouldn't go on a psychedelic trip with them either.

No matter what, your trip should include people. Solo tripping is only recommended for the very experienced and introverted. The people with you when you trip should be people you trust, who make you laugh, that you care about. Taking a psychedelic trip together is a type of intimacy.

Trip with people you trust. When your masks fall off, you should be with people you feel comfortable seeing you that way. It is difficult to derive value from a trip if you spend the experience trying to build new masks to protect yourself from the people around you. Trust will allow you to experience the strangeness together, without a second thought. Letting go of some of those second thoughts (or third thoughts) allows for greater exploration of your mind.

Trip with people who make you laugh. Once a friend of mine and I were coming up on LSD and chatting in the kitchen. He misheard something I said and asked if I was talking about soccer. Instead of denying it, I agreed and riffed that the soccer was played only by dogs. With each response, we tried to make the idea just a little bit weirder. Back and forth we went, making each other laugh. We laughed so hard our faces started to hurt. We decided that the part that hurt the most from all this laughing was the very top of our heads. Eventually, our companions came to the kitchen to figure out what we were laughing about. They found us holding the tops of our heads and laughing while intermittently saying "ow!" When directly asked what was so funny, we both said, "Chihuahuas playing soccer in Argentina!" I no longer remember everything we invented or why it was so funny, but I will never forget how good it felt to trip with that friend.

Trip with people you care about. You will be sharing a significant experience with your companions. It will most likely create a sense of bonding. Your experience will be deeper and more meaningful if you share it with people that you care about.

Where should your first trip be? The obvious first choice is to trip in your home or the home of one of your companions. A good place to trip should follow these guidelines: No social intrusions, enough space for the group, and maybe a decent audio visual system.

There shouldn't be any residents of that home that are not a part of the experience. In addition, you should be able to guarantee that no one will drop by. Social intrusions are exceptionally disruptive and can derail an entire experience. Together, everyone on the trip will build what is essentially a new consensual reality. Social intrusions bring a new viewpoint that is not steeped in the formulation of your trip and can reshape reality in disconcerting ways.

You should have enough space that everyone can comfortably lounge. It's likely that everyone will want to be horizontal at some point. It is best to provide an environment that makes it possible. Sometimes people get antsy, so it is good to have enough space for people to walk around a bit. Sometimes people experience gastro-intestinal distress. It is best to have enough bathrooms!

Music will probably be an important part of your environment. Having a decent sound system will significantly improve your experience. Coming down from a trip can be easier with a good movie. I highly recommend tripping in a space with a TV.

If you or your companions do not have access to a space that meets these guidelines, Airbnb is now an option. Make sure that you have the entire space and that space is private. Renting a space can also be useful if you are traveling to trip with someone special, if you just want to be in a space that doesn't remind you of the responsibilities of regular life, or if you'd like to trip someplace with additional luxuries like a fireplace or hot tub.

Once you have a couple of trips under your belt, public spaces can be quite enjoyable, given appropriate precautions. Festivals like Burning Man or Coachella are popular places to trip, and tripping at museums is a perennial favorite.

When contemplating tripping in public, consider what people and systems you will have to interact with. Do not assume that you will feel comfortable doing things that ordinarily feel safe and normal like riding the subway, buying a soda at the convenience store, or even crossing a busy street. These behaviors that we have learned and stuffed into our subconscious are not guaranteed to function as normal. Tripping in public places can be very rewarding, but should only be undertaken after you have some experience with the drug you are using and with someone acting as Ground Control.

When tripping in public, it is also advisable

to take a "museum dose." Museums are great fun while tripping as psychedelics heighten your appreciation of art and ideas. However, they become much less fun if you are too high. "Threshold dose" or a quantity of psychedelic that becomes just perceptible is ideal. As dosage may vary per person, it may take a few trips to determine what your threshold dose is. I recommend not tripping in public until you have been able to determine what that dose is for you.

I once took a museum dose of LSD with a couple of companions while my designated driver cruised down Lake Shore Drive. We went to the Field Museum, arriving as they opened in the morning on a quiet weekday. Our Ground Control managed purchasing the tickets and we broke into two groups. My companion and I wandered through the special exhibit about lava. (There were lava lamps in the pedestal of every table, not visible unless you are of child height or, like me, a tripper obsessed with the underneaths of things.) Then we went on to the exhibit on Tibet. A poorly marked staircase that wasn't actually open to the public led us to a storeroom full of ancient dioramas. After we realized our mistake and momentarily panicked, we managed to exit without detection. In a section about geography, we were eyed by a security guard. All of a sudden, I became aware of how abnormally I was acting. But then I realized that it didn't matter; being silly in public isn't actually against the rules.

My favorite museum trip was to the Metropolitan Museum of Art in New York City where I was utterly transfixed by Alphonse Mucha's "Joan of Arc." Acting outside of society's norms can garner dirty looks, but being weird isn't a crime. It's ok to look underneath things, play hopscotch on a map tiled into the floor, or cry from the beauty of a painting, even in public.

Tripping in a noisy apartment or in public is an undeniable aspect of an urban trip, and there are also many interesting experiences to be had in a rural setting. For your first few trips, it is advisable to trip in the type of environment that you feel most comfortable. People tend to be more comfortable in whichever is more familiar to them. Urbanites who never go camping can find rural spaces intimidating. Those more accustomed to rural or small town environments can likewise find major metropolitan spaces overwhelming.

Excellent rural environments include campgrounds or private spaces. The key is finding a spot where you aren't tripping a few feet away from a family out for a weekend at the park. There is so much wonder to be found in natural environments. The most beautiful things I have ever seen were the full moon on a cloudless night, the patterns on a leaf, and the dancing flames of a campfire. The only downside of heading into the wilderness is a lack of plumbing.

Tripping outdoors can also facilitate that sense of connectedness that is so often generated from the psychedelic experience. It is so easy to sense how connected we are to the earth and everything else living on its surface when your fingers and toes are interlaced with the grass and your body is covered by the dappled light filtered through the trees.

A group of my friends once held a camping trip on a piece of land sandwiched between a forest and cropland. We had access to ten acres of forest and prairie with a building in the center outfitted with plumbing and electricity. Walking around felt like we'd been transported to a magical land. The trees breathed and the creek spoke and the flowers danced. At some point, I acquired a carrot of extraordinary size which became both a magic wand and a snack. The blue sky shimmered and the dark earth hummed. In the evening, we danced and drummed around a fire before sleeping under the stars.

Sometimes a tinge of darkness can seep into a trip without having a useful experience attached. In these cases, a slight adjustment of your set or setting will usually resolve the situation. This type of darkness can be brought in through foreboding music, in which case, change the tunes. Or maybe something you saw created a strong suggestion for distressing visuals. Go to a different area and ask your companions to engage you on a positive topic. Tell your companions what you are experiencing and don't be afraid to ask for help. Be mindful of your setting. Who you are with and where you are has an enormous impact on your experience.

Substance

Finally, the drugs that you take will impact your experience. It is vital that you know your substance and know your source. Be utterly confident that you are taking what and how much you think you are taking. Consuming unknown chemicals at unknown dosages is very dangerous.

I will be addressing the basics of classic psychedelics and common companion drugs. This book is not intended to be a primer on chemical substances. Before consuming any psychoactive drug, I recommend looking it up on Erowid. org. Erowid is the world's largest database of psychoactives. They are committed to providing accurate information without judgment and are the most valuable resource available to you as you determine your substance.

The most common of the classic psychedelics are magic mushrooms. They are the easiest to acquire as they are the easiest to manufacture. However, they are also the most variable in their effects. Potencies vary significantly between species and individual mushrooms. Effects vary significantly based on an individual's personal chemistry. A dose of dried mushrooms varies from one-tenth of a gram to five grams. Fresh, that range is from one to fifty grams. Onset could happen in as little as ten minutes or take just over an hour. A mushroom trip can last anywhere from four to ten hours. Try eating a slightly smaller dose than you think is a good amount and wait an hour. At that point, you might decide to nibble a little bit more.

LSD is much harder to manufacture and therefore much harder to acquire. However, it is far more predictable in its effects. Dosages range from 50-400 micrograms, with the smaller dose providing a threshold, or barely perceptible high.

More LSD will make you higher until you reach
about 400 micrograms. Exceeding 400 micrograms results in diminishing returns. Onset
happens between a half hour to an hour after
ingestion. A threshold dose will last approximately 10 hours, while higher doses will last up
to 16 hours.

Mescaline, the active ingredient in peyote, is
rarely available outside of the regions where
it is grown. Like mushrooms, peyote dosage
varies greatly depending on the plant. Often,
mescaline is extracted from the peyote. A dose
of the extracted mescaline varies depending on
the method of extraction, but a standard dose
is between two to three hundred milligrams. A
mescaline trip lasts approximately eight hours,
and comes with a good chance of vomiting or
gastric-intestinal distress during onset.

5meoDMT (otherwise known as The Toad) is
a classic psychedelic in its own right, though
it can be combined with other psychedelics.
5meoDMT is not orally active, so it is usually
vaporized (1-20 mg) or insufflated (snorted,
3-25 mg). The effects last for five minutes to
an hour depending on quantity and method of
consumption with vaporization producing faster
and stronger effects.

DMT is another short acting psychedelic that isn't orally active unless it is combined with an MAOI, such as in Ayahuasca. DMT itself is only active when insufflated or vaporized. Vaporization of 2 to 50 milligrams creates a 15-20 minute long trip.

The 2C class of psychedelic phenethylamines were designed in the late 1970's by Alexander Shulgan. There are several variations including 2cB (Nexus), 2ct7 (Blue Mystic), and others. Each variety comes with unique dosage recommendations and durations. If trying these substances for the first time, it is crucial to use the lowest recommended dose as a small percentage of people become extraordinarily high on what would be a threshold dose for anyone else.

There are many opinions about the differences in the qualitative experiences between the classic psychedelics. Many people claim that each substance produces a significantly different experience. Others claim that a double blind trial would yield no differentiation between substances. My opinion is that while substantially similar, each substance brings a certain "flavor" to your experience.

Another way to flavor your experience is to include companion drugs. I recommend never using a companion drug until you are past the peak of your experience, and never try a new drug while on your first experience with another one.

The most common companion drug is alcohol. At the height of a trip, alcohol may have little to no discernible effects unless you consume a great quantity of it. While the flavor of a beer may be very pleasant while tripping, do not get drunk. It is a very unpleasant experience for you and everyone around you. However, when you get to the end of your trip, it can be very relaxing to wind down with a drink.

The next most common companion drug is marijuana. Like alcohol, do not use it heavily during the trip, but a little at the end can be quite nice for those already familiar with its effects.

Nitrous oxide has intensely synergistic effects with psychedelics. It is easy to acquire and provides a boost to your trip that produces visuals and a sense of intensity. On the flip side, it also produces an intense and immediate physical addiction that is quite unpleasant. In addition, it can take a little while to shake off the mind numbing haze that nitrous induces.

A friend of mine had retrofitted some scuba gear to dispense nitrous oxide instead of air. This is when I learned that my body processes N2O differently from other people. I would take a hit while walking and then get someone else to alternate hits with me. When they fell down, I'd find someone else to replace them. "One for me, one for you, one for me, one for you, one for me, whoopsie there, hey you, yeah you, one for me, one for you…" Unlike me, you should be prepared to at least sit down while consuming nitrous.

A similar dissociative is ketamine. Ketamine is much harder to acquire and has a much stronger synergistic effect than nitrous. It has a similar short-term addictive quality which is much more powerful when it is used on its own. If using ketamine with a psychedelic, make sure that you have a comfortable place to lie down. The experience is highly internalized as your body becomes somewhat numb while your mind travels the kaleidoscope. The intensity of a ketamine trip is predicated on dosage, which can run from 10 to 100 milligrams.

Combining the entheogen MDMA (Ecstasy) with a classic psychedelic is common. MDMA forces your body to excrete serotonin, which creates a very positive mental state. It also has a stimulant effect. Many people enjoy this for dancing all night long or inducing cuddle piles.

Dosages can run from 30 to 200 milligrams, with 75-100 mg being the most common. It can cause some muscle clenching (especially on higher doses), so I recommend taking it with magnesium salicylate (Doans), an OTC NSAID used for back pain.

Do not combine psychedelics with stimulants. They already have a stimulant-like effect. Adding a stimulant to psychedelics can cause erratic behavior, time loss, and thought loops, which can be very unpleasant.

Natural Landmarks

Without the context of experience, describing the psychedelic landscape can sound incomprehensible, hokey, or even insane. It's like describing a flavor to someone who has never tasted it. While you can describe how salty or sweet, fatty or umami a flavor is, at some point you begin to mention hints of berry or the woodiness of cinnamon. It only makes sense if you have a common frame of reference.

I think it is most accurate to use "sensory saturation" to describe a lot of what we call psychedelic hallucinations. You will not experience a virtual reality or dream world type hallucination outside of very specific chemical states that require very large doses. What you will experience is more analogous to filter effects caused by the hallucinogen generating random signal noise in your brain. Colors will become more saturated and lean toward the classic "psychedelic" color palette. Geometric patterns (especially grids and spirals) will make reality look like an optical illusion. After-images will persist, creating trails that follow movement. The closest representation that I've ever seen of psychedelic visuals are the images created by Google's AI Deep Dream, which was created to help software engineers understand how neural networks process visual information. These images are reminiscent of psychedelic visuals not only for the intensified colors, but also for the inclusion of suggestive interpretations hidden in random patterns.

The human mind is a pattern recognition machine. This function will be heightened when on psychedelics. Faces, figures, or movement may emerge from art. Music gains a completeness and can produce synesthesia (you may see the music as colors). Ideas freely associate in ways that produce fascinating thought structures, from absurdist comedy to revelatory insight.

When we think, our brain insulates the pathways that we have used, making it easier to think that same thought in the future. If we stop thinking that thought, our brain will capture the insulation from those pathways and repurpose it for the thoughts we are currently thinking. This has the actual, physical effect of thoughts wearing paths in our brains the way our feet wear paths in the forest. Part of the magic of the psychedelic experience is that it makes trailblazing in our minds so much easier. We have more freedom to think new thoughts.

Psychedelics activate serotonin receptors in our brains while simultaneously diminishing activity in the areas responsible for our default mode network. This is the network of brain areas that increase in activity when we are not focused on something outside ourselves, and may be the network responsible for the sense of separate self. The quieting of this area of the brain is analogous to snow falling on the pathways of your mental forest. It becomes much easier to travel on a new path, and you may not even be able to recognize the well-worn path you usually tread. Creative thinking becomes not only easier, but unavoidable.

This also allows us to bypass the assumptions and dismissals our sober mind makes as we move through our days. Instead of seeing a tree and dismissing it as something we understand and can comfortably ignore, our brain takes a different path and notices, really notices the tree as if for the first time. You may become aware of the delicate texture of the bark or the sound of the breeze through the leaves, or just how much space the tree takes up. These are all things that you know, but may not have taken time to appreciate. Each of these moments where

you become fundamentally aware of something
so mundane that it never broaches conscious
thought can bring a sense of awe: awe at the
delicate beauty you see, awe of the majestic
sounds you hear, awe from feeling connected to
everything around you.

Feeling awe may be the most useful aspect of a
psychedelic trip. It stimulates personal growth
by increasing our feelings of empathy, com-
passion, altruism, and well-being. The effects
of experiencing a deep sense of awe are often
prolonged happiness, increased critical thinking,
and improved health. It can help you fall in love
with being alive because nothing makes being
alive better than engaging with it.

All of these mental effects produce the experiences that are common among trippers. They are
so common, in fact, that the psychedelic community has developed jargon to describe them.

Disillusionment of Ego

The most common of these is referred to as ego
disillusionment. An ego, which in this context
refers to the conscious sense of self, consists of
an internal monologue combined with a predictive model of reactions and a sense of separate-
ness from everything external. Each individual's

sense of self is not as consistent as it seems to be. When neural plasticity increases and your default mode network becomes less active, internal monologues can fade away. Your predictive model for how you expect to react to stimuli may prove false. Your sense of connectedness to everything around you will intensify.

How attached are you to your persona? How much comfort do you derive from who you think you are or who you wish yourself to be? Is your sense of self constructed of personal edicts designed to define the boundaries of who you are? Do you keep yourself under control? As your ego begins to dissolve, it is imperative that you surrender each of these controls that you place upon yourself. As paradoxical as it sounds, fighting disillusionment is ultimately fighting yourself. Such a battle is very unpleasant, whereas letting go of your sense of self and experiencing the moment free of ego is a great pleasure.

A common place to explore the ego and its disillusionment is the mirror. While gazing into the mirror may sound narcissistic, it can be intensely introspective. My personal journeys into the mirror have shown me my face with overlaid alternate versions of myself: the maiden, the mother, the crone, and the beast. Some people have seen the masks that they make for themselves and the cracks that lead them to question the utility of those masks. Others see ever-changing emotions. Be aware that the mirror is a powerful experience, but don't be afraid of what it holds.

The Other

While many psychedelic experiences contain ego loss, some involve discovering The Other. It is possible to encounter a sense of another presence that you can communicate with telepathically that embodies an archetype. While this can sound hokey, it is an experience that is not only common among psychedelic users, but of spiritually minded people throughout history. The Other is often interpreted as some powerful, other dimensional being, some sort of god. There is invariably some sort of knowledge held by The Other that the tripper is challenged to successfully interpret. My very first psychedelic experience involved an interaction with The Other in the form of the full moon. I worshiped her. She told me no. It initiated years of exploration of my personal relationship with the god image. Sometimes the otherness is plural. When encountering a group of Others, they are usually described as elves or aliens. These elves are often mischievous, but are less communicative than

The Other. You can imagine The Other and The Elves as a dream-like overlay on reality.

The Landscape

This overlay can also manifest as a landscape, especially when you close your eyes. These landscapes are sensed in the way that you can sense the presence of the ocean with your eyes closed. Your mind fills in ideas about its size, weight, and power. Similarly, the feelings of these landscapes can overwhelm your interpretations of your physical environment, especially when your eyes are closed. There are three landscapes that commonly present in a psychedelic experience: the dome, the vista, and the void. The dome exists as a bubble or a habitable zone, often populated by elves. The vista is an awareness of how much reality there is, like standing at the edge of a cliff and feeling how far existence spreads. The void is the awareness of an infinity of nothingness, as though you exist in the emptiness between the stars.

Epiphanies

Also among these common experiences are epiphanies. These epiphanies can sound very simple when shared with another person, but represent a significant increase of understanding about how someone approaches life. These epiphanies bear a strong resemblance to those that come out of Post Traumatic Growth, only without the trauma. They lead to a greater appreciation of life, an increased ability to relate to others, a sense of personal strength, an awareness of new possibilities, or a deepening of your spiritual or philosophical ideology.

The most common epiphany is a sense of connectedness with all living things. This is accompanied by feelings of belonging and love, that we are all a part of something larger than an individual. This can bring an urge to be kind to others as they are now seen as being all of the same tribe of humanity. Another common epiphany is how small we are compared to the world or even the universe. This may make someone feel like their problems aren't as big as they'd imagined or that pressures to be different from their authentic self are meaningless. Many epiphanies lead to realizing how much agency we have in choosing our own happiness. What they all have in common is a deep sense of profundity.

While these experiences are common on trips, they do not come up on every trip. It is possible to encourage a type of experience through intention, but psychedelic experiences can only be guided, not driven. Knowing about these natural landmarks will help you guide a trip, but none of them can be summoned on demand.

Preparing for a Trip

All psychoactive substances should be treated with respect. Preparing for your trip will not only keep you safe, it will maximize your enjoyment of the experience. The section on **Setting** has already covered the basics. This section specifically focuses on experiences in a private location, with a carefully chosen guest list, with the goal of exploration of the psychedelic space. While these ideas are often applicable and useful to other scenarios, they will be explored under that context.

Timeline

There is an arc to the psychedelic experience. Between anticipation on the front end and integration afterwards, an experience unfolds in five phases: onset, peaking, the plateau, coming down, and mostly sober. The duration of this arc is affected by which substance you ingest. To prepare for your trip, it is useful to understand this timeline.

Onset

Onset, sometimes called coming up, begins as soon as the drug hits your bloodstream. The method of ingestion, the type of substance, and how much food is in your stomach will affect how much time you have between ingestion and onset. Onset is your transition from normal reality to the psychedelic space. It can feel like butterflies in your stomach that transform into a rocket ship. It can feel like a gradual increase in the saturation of your senses.

Onset is mostly waiting. You're waiting to arrive in the psychedelic space, waiting to see how far the drugs will take you. Depending on the substance and mode of ingestion, onset can take a few minutes or a few hours. However long it lasts, you can make use of it. This time of transition is a time of acclimation in which you can complete your mental and physical preparations.

Mental preparation during onset involves revisiting the intentions that you have brought to this trip and sharing them with the people you will be tripping with. The previous chapter discussed intention: you should develop your intention before you dose. During onset, meditate on that intention. Sharing that intention (to the degree to which you are comfortable) with the people tripping with you adds gravity to it. It does this by forcing you to articulate your intention with words and by recruiting your fellow trippers as a support structure. You in turn will be able to support the intentions of your companions if you know what they are.

The group that I did most of my explorations with would begin each trip with an opening circle. As soon as everyone had received their dose (or not if they were Ground Control), we would sit in a circle. One person would bring a stick (usually a drumstick, but any object that can be comfortably held and seen works). This was the Talking Stick. Once the person with the stick invoked the ceremony, no one was allowed to talk unless they held the stick. The person with the stick would share their intentions with the circle. These intentions could be anything: contemplation of a particular idea, discovery of where the trip would lead, to experience awe with friends, or to support the journeys of others. Once a person had shared their intentions, the stick would be passed to their neighbor. The sharing of intentions would continue until the stick had returned to the first person and the ceremony was concluded.

When you are tripping as a pair, the Talking Stick loses its usefulness, but it is still important to have a conversation about intention as you are coming up, even if the other person in your pair is Ground Control.

Tripping is not purely a mental exercise. It is a full body experience. There are lots of little tricks that you can use to acclimate your body. Most people choose an outfit for the experience. It should be something comfortable that you can lounge or stretch in with no aspects that feel restricting. Choose textures, colors, and patterns that you find pleasurable. Wear something that feels fun, or matches your intention.

Tactile experiences can ease the physical transition and feel especially pleasurable. I love to take a shower during onset when possible. A friend of mine introduced me to brushing my teeth during onset, and I've made a point to do so at the beginning of every trip. Many people enjoy light physical activity like dancing or yoga. You are likely to experience a mild stimulant effect, especially on LSD. However, your balance will also be slightly affected. It may feel good to move, but keep the acrobatics to a minimum.

You may begin to see a glow emanating from everything. Visual and auditory details may intensify and replicate. Anything you perceive through your senses may trigger an emotional response. It is common to sense that the world around you is breathing. The familiar will become novel. Your patterns of thinking will become more fluid.

The Peak

The peak is the most intense part of your trip. This stage is characterized by sensory saturation, dynamic thinking, and possibly ego loss. All of the characteristics of the peak are symptoms of a mind coping with a brain that is trying to temporarily disable all of the personal settings that you've developed over your lifetime. This return to a childlike state may produce a sense of wonder and joy as your mind freshly interprets the way you perceive reality.

You may experience ego loss and begin to feel anxiety or a desire to hold firm to your sense of self. If that happens, remember that this is the moment of the greatest power and benefit of the psychedelic trip. Let go of your concerns for the future, or how you are perceived, or any other messages emanating from your internal dialog. Focus on the moment. Focus on your breath. Trust that you are safe in the setting you have created with intention. If you can find this opportunity and surrender your ego, you may experience the transcendent bliss that is the deepest magic of the psychedelic experience.

The Plateau

After the peak comes the plateau. This is a time of comfortable highness where time means much less than it usually does. Depending on set, setting, and substance, you and your companions may have quieted down, snuggled in, and become introspective during the peak. Post peak, you will likely become more conversational and seek out interactions and experiences.

During the plateau, revel in the companionship and small pleasures around you. Let your conversation flow outside of your comfort zone. Blow your mind with a bite of mango sorbet. Rediscover fingerpainting. Engage in something creative, tactile, experiential. If possible, go outside and enjoy nature. Something as commonplace as the sky, the moon, a tree, can be breathtakingly beautiful. Follow the joy inherent in the experience. Have fun!

At this stage, you may choose to introduce any of the companion drugs mentioned in the section on substance. These will have their own timelines that will work within that of the primary psychedelic. Remember that you are still high and should be careful with the doses with any companion drug. Start small and see what happens.

Coming Down

After the plateau, as your body breaks down the drugs, you will come down. Your brain has been working overtime to produce the amazing experience that you are wrapping up. It will begin to feel a bit sluggish. Be kind and don't try to push your mind too hard.

You may be hungry during this stage. More on this in the menu section. You will probably feel tired, but not necessarily sleepy. This is a transitional phase where your mind returns to sobriety.

Down, but not ready to sleep

Some people can end a psychedelic trip and totter off to bed, falling into a deep and blissful sleep. Do not assume that you or your companions will be able to manage that transition gracefully: plan ahead. I highly recommend having a movie (or two) chosen beforehand. Choose something witty, weird, or beautiful. Popcorn action flicks do not usually shine in this context. Likewise, avoid powerful dramas or depressing themes. Your trip will have brought you intense feelings of joy and awe that should be fostered to enhance the whole experience.

Many people, especially those who otherwise experience insomnia, use a mild sedative to help them get to sleep after a trip. Regardless of how early you dose, it takes a good night's sleep to bookend a psychedelic trip. Some people prefer to dose later in the day as bright sunlight can be overwhelming to eyes dilated by a drug. When choosing the time to ingest your psychedelic, consider how long the trip will take and how late you are willing to stay up. The experience will be intense and the day after will require rest and integration, which is much more difficult (and less constructive) if you have wildly departed from your regular sleep schedule.

The Menu

Classic psychedelic trips can take from 4-16 hours depending on the substance and dosage. They universally inhibit appetite. It is important to plan ahead for your body's needs before dosing. The experience of eating and drinking can also be extremely pleasurable as your appetite returns.

Taking a psychedelic trip is a special occasion. It is especially useful as a rare and intentional departure from the mundane. Psychedelic experiences, especially if you are a novice, are affected by the subjective expansion of time, much like when you go on vacation to a new place. Our brains devote more resources to novel experiences, making a trip seem much longer than it actually takes to experience it. Marking this experience with your favorite foods enhances the significance of the trip.

You're unlikely to be hungry for the first few hours of any trip, so it is important to fuel up beforehand. However, many psychedelics produce gastrointestinal distress during onset. For psychedelics with higher instances of nausea, eat something easily digestible like a protein shake an hour before dosing. For psychedelics with lower instances of nausea, just make sure that you've eaten something light and healthy.

Be sure to have filtered or distilled water on hand as residual flavors in tap water can be distracting. Get your favorite drinks and have several on hand. Minimize (but don't necessarily exclude) alcohol, caffeine, and sugar. Common favorites include fruit juices and carbonated water. My personal favorite drinks for a trip are dry rhubarb soda and cherry lambic beer. Both are a little sour and a little sweet. The lambic is 4% alcohol and too intense in flavor to drink quickly. While I don't recommend any significant quantity of alcohol during a trip, you may wish to have your favorite beer or wine on hand for when you've come down.

At some point, you may start to get hungry, but you will probably only want a few bites. During this phase, having small, delicious (especially juicy) snacks around is particularly fun. Keep it simple and minimize the need for preparation. Most people enjoy fruit. I had a companion who would bring a cantaloupe to every trip, and the texture and juiciness never failed to be transcendent. Prepare your fruits as necessary beforehand, as doing it during your first trip can be surprisingly daunting. The key is to choose foods that feel wholesome.

At the end of your trip you will be ready for something resembling an actual meal, but you will probably not want to make it. You will definitely not want to go out to get it. It is also likely that you will not want to get delivery. Be prepared and have something ready to go, preferably something that is relatively gentle on your stomach. Nearly every psychonaut that I have ever known swears by soup at the end of a trip. A companion of mine used to make a pot of Manischewitz Split Pea Soup from a packet, and it was divinity in a bowl. I recommend having your favorite soup made up and ready to heat before you begin your trip. Soup isn't strictly required, though it is a common favorite. What is most important is that you have a plan in place before you begin your trip.

Prepare the Space

It is important to prepare the space in which you will trip. When preparing your home or other space for a trip it should be clean, have a nest, and be properly lit.

Put away all mundane distractions by tidying the space as much as possible. Clean the visual and functional space, even if that means shoving items in a closet somewhere. It isn't just going to be the location of a party, it's going to be your spaceship into the cosmos. Give the kitchen and bathrooms the most thorough cleaning possible. Your tripping mind will notice things that your sober mind glosses over. You don't want to end up getting lost in the details of a dirty sink. Many people tripping at home also choose to light incense a few hours beforehand so that their home has a slightly different smell than usual, to create a signifier that the space has been prepared for a unique experience.

Make the floor inviting. You can significantly improve an experience by providing a nest, or a place where everyone can comfortably lounge on the floor. I like to fill the largest, most open space in my house with a futon and bean bags and every pillow I own. Unlike a cocktail party, you won't be standing around or sitting on couches enjoying casual conversation. You will want to sit and stretch and roll around.

Your eyes will be dilated and light will therefore be brighter. Provide low ambient lighting for all spaces (even the bathroom) so that no one will have to operate light switches for overhead lights during the trip. If you are tripping during a sunny day, shade the windows.

If your trip is out in the world, you'll want to prepare the space that you return to at the end. Make sure that you have a tidy space to come down in and fresh sheets on your bed to sleep in.

If you are tripping outside, many of these ideas still apply. A picnic blanket and pillows in a shady spot can be an excellent nest.

Soundscape

When tripping indoors, build a soundscape to offset urban distractions and to provide a landscape for introspection. Curate a selection before you trip so that you don't have to combat an empty soundscape populated with only the hum of a refrigerator and the swoosh of passing cars while you search through a musical database. You can choose music mid-trip, but you should have appropriate music ready.

Music can help ease you into the psychedelic space. Have a playlist of ambient music that allows conversation and will last you through the majority of the trip. I default to downtempo, trip-hop, dub, space rock, and dream pop. Other common favorites include world music and classical music. Simple music like most pop rock or less complicated styles of electronic dance music are less likely to produce the desired effect.

Music festivals and large gatherings with significant sound systems are amazing, but for smaller outdoor gatherings, recorded music will often pale in comparison with the natural soundscape.

Helpful Tools

When tripping inside, I like to provide some activities to engage with throughout the trip. These activities often occupy the eyes or hands just as the soundscape occupies the ears. They are not necessary, but can help trippers engage with the experience.

High resolution art books are often fun to look at while talking to a companion. Intricate images give your mind something to build heightened visuals with. The works of MC Escher, Georgia O'Keeffe, Van Gogh, Frida Kahlo, and Alex Grey, as well as Tibetan mandalas, Islamic patterns, and nature photography, are good for this. Art books are expensive though, so you may want to get them from the library.

Keep some art supplies handy. Many adults find them intimidating, but only because they are focused on the result rather than the experience. Watercolors and inks are marvelous for watching pigment flow through water and blend on a page. Watercolor markers and pencils make the experience more accessible. As a bonus, they can be used as body paints. My personal favorite is to dip watercolor pencils in water and then doodle on my friends.

Fiddle toys can be useful for managing any awkward energy someone may feel while coming up. Satisfying fiddle toys have become more and more accessible, but I still prefer old fashioned ones like silly putty or juggling balls.

Keep eye masks or eye pillows on hand. Depending on where the drug takes you, it may be enjoyable to lie back blindfolded to pay attention to your mind's eye for a while.

The Five Rules of Tripping

The five rules of tripping were part of psyche-delic culture long before I arrived on the scene. Being a cultural artifact, they can change from subculture to subculture. Regardless of their specifics, they all have the same purpose: to help you bridge the gap between everyday life and the psychedelic space.

We take psychedelics to alter our consciousness, to get high, to dance with the fairies. To do this, we must let go of our filters, our automatic behaviors, and our assumptions. These filters are essential for everyday life, so when we shed them, we need a safety net to protect us. These five rules are that net.

Rule # 1: Turn off your phone.

Rule #2: Don't go out without ground control.

Rule #3: Don't cut your hair.

Rule #4: You cannot fly.

Rule #5: You will come down.

Turn Off Your Phone

When this rule was created, it referred to unplugging your landline. Now, it means a little bit more than just powering down your smartphone. It is shorthand for setting aside time where you will not be communicating with anyone who is not tripping with you. Don't connect with anyone who is not sharing your experience. Don't let anything outside of the experience contact you through notifications of any type. This is important because communication into and out of the psychedelic space is confusing and stressful.

While in the psychedelic space your mental filters will be down. Using a communication device will no longer be effortless. Screens will develop unfathomable depths. Calling your mom will create a wild conversation that you have no control over, may make you feel quite uncomfortable, and could scare the hell out of her. Ordering a pizza will feel like a monumental task involving interaction with aliens.

Preventing communication from anyone outside of the psychedelic space is the best way to respect the power of the situation. It is also an excellent way to respect the time and attention of your companions in much the same way we do at the theater or dinner table.

Don't Go Out Without Ground Control

You have intentionally plasticized your brain. Routine social interactions (buying a soda pop at the convenience store, waving hi to your neighbor, etc.) are built out of a million little ingrained behaviors that can fall apart at inopportune moments.

Once when I acted as Ground Control for a friend, he decided that it was time to walk from his apartment to his friend's. It was only a few blocks. We had discussed this possibility beforehand and they knew to expect both him and his state of mind. Our walk took us across an intersection of a busy road that had two through lanes and two turning lanes of traffic in both directions. My friend saw a car stopped in the lane closest to us and began to cross the street. Unfortunately, that car was just waiting to make a right turn and he was about to walk into traffic. I ran out behind him and pulled him back while he looked at me incredulously and asked "What?!" He had picked up on a single clue that we use to know if it is safe to cross the road, but had ignored the cross light. I made him hold my hand for the rest of our walk.

I'm not trying to scare you from venturing out into the world at all, just to illustrate how taking psychedelics can temporarily disrupt ingrained behaviors. This can be an exceptionally useful and charming aspect of taking psychedelics, but you must respect the risks it entails. My friend knew this and was following the rules. That's why I was with him. If your trip plan requires venturing out (attending a concert, visiting a museum, and night hiking being my personal favorites) bring a sober friend to accompany you.

Do Not Cut Your Hair

This rule is essentially the same as "In vino veritas, in aqua sanitas", i.e., "In wine there is truth, in water there is good sense." Refrain from making significant decisions in a state of altered consciousness—make sure you have considered it when sober before committing to it. This could be a decision about getting bangs or a decision to initiate an intimate relationship.

It's not that you shouldn't have sex on psyche-delics. Sex on psychedelics can be magical. It can also be awkward. But most importantly, you should decide what your personal boundaries are for intimate contact before you take drugs, and stick to it when you're high.

There are many different cultural, subcultural, and personal responses to touch. Humans use touch to connect with the people around them, to show affection, and to express support. It is very likely that you or your companions will wish to touch and/or be touched during the course of your experience. This will be far more comfortable and produce the desired effect if everyone in your group understands each other's boundaries. This does not necessarily mean that an explicit conversation is required, but depending on the group, it might be useful.

You Cannot Fly

Believing that you can fly while on psychedelics is an urban myth that evolved from the fear-mongering of the 70's, as society went through a backlash against the 60's. This rule is a flippant reminder that you may interpret reality and your abilities in a novel light, but reality doesn't care how high you are. Sometimes this rule is known as, "You are not god."

Euphoria or an experience of revelation while high can engender a sense that more is possible while high than you had previously assumed. In some sense, this is true. Creative thought is heightened, for example. But this does not change any of your limitations as a human. Getting high will not make you better than anyone else and it will not negate the laws of physics. In short: if you could fly, you would be able to take off from the ground. Don't jump off a cliff (physical or metaphorical) to prove otherwise.

You Will Come Down

Like all things, this too shall pass. When time loses meaning, it can feel as though you will trip forever. This can bring anxiety about time and how it applies to you as you question if you will ever come down. It is surprisingly useful to know that even if you can't connect with time, time will never lose track of you.

If the trip is not going well (refer to "setting" for advice on how to prevent or adapt to that), it can be comforting to remember that the drug in your system will always break down and, eventually, you will come down. It is inevitable.

Integration

Taking time to integrate your experience is crucial. It is how you can bring the benefits of the heightened experience back with you while you resume the normal cycles of your life. Not taking the time to make this transition robs the experience of its transformative power and could even result in cognitive dissonance if you carry insights from your experience around in your mind without integrating those ideas into the full context of your ordinary life . The magic can only translate into reality if we take the time to integrate it.

When planning a psychedelic trip, schedule at least one day afterwards to rest, recover, and integrate. While it may take months to fully integrate a psychedelic experience, the following day or two are crucial for soberly considering how you can benefit from the profound moments it contained. You need time to let your sober brain reflect on your experience with altered consciousness. And, entering a trip with the knowledge that you will have time to integrate it will significantly reduce any anxiety you may feel about surrendering to the moment. No matter how far out you travel, you must have time to return.

Begin the integration period with time in contemplation. Go for a walk somewhere that isn't overstimulating. Hiking through the woods is an inherently contemplative action. You are away from the distractions of modern life and it minimizes the need to react to your environment. Movement energizes and occupies your body, allowing for free thought. If hiking in the woods is impossible or unappealing, find some other way to give yourself time to think away from distractions. Take a walk, ride a bike, draw, or simply sit in meditation.

Spend this time alone or with the people who shared your trip. Give yourself time before you have to reapply the masks of daily social interaction. Your experience removed some of these masks. Allow yourself time to experience your sense of self without them.

Talk to your companions or write about your experience. The important thing is that you build a narrative that helps you understand and retain your experience. Talk or write about what you remember most, what was most interesting, what surprised you. Follow the ideas that still speak to you, explore them as far as you can go. See where your memories of your trip lead to ideas about yourself and your relationships.

Test out your new ideas. How has the experience impacted you? How can you use that to improve your daily life? What does this tell you about your goals and how you've been pursuing them? What have you learned about your priorities and how that impacts your behavior? How can you live your life true to yourself? How can you use your experience to engender growth?

Pay attention to your feelings. Habitual thoughts may have been disrupted. What do your feelings have to say about them now? Do any of those usual thoughts feel like they need to be re-examined? Have your beliefs been challenged? What do you believe now? Are your beliefs useful?

New paths have been forged in your brain. Which ones do you choose to tread? Are they familiar paths or new ones? Intentionally re-tread the paths that you have consciously chosen. Reinforce your chosen mental pathways by thinking them through. Journaling or taking time out of each day to process these thoughts will yield great results.

Be wary of extreme changes and absolutist

philosophies. Sometimes, a psychedelic experience will break us out of a destructive behavior and give us an opportunity to let go of our attachment to that behavior. At other times when we recognize how far from our true self we usually live, we can swing like a pendulum in the opposite direction, well past a reasonable, healthy new goal. Signs of this can be found when we disregard common sense or become fanatical in our worldview. If you find yourself contemplating an extreme lifestyle change, check in with someone you trust who you know has your best interests at heart. Besides, if you have had a fundamentally transformative experience, having someone in your corner to support you as you make big changes in your life will improve your chances of making those changes successfully.

Be gentle with your body. Get good rest before returning to your regularly scheduled life. Eat well. Exercise. Prepare yourself to reenter your regular life centered and energized. Treasure the mindfulness and insight that your experience has provided.

How to be Ground Control

Ground Control, as we have seen, are the people who accompany trippers while staying sober. They are important to support trippers who have minimal experience, solo trippers, or to facilitate interactions with public spaces.

When acting as Ground Control for people who have never tripped before, your job is to be reassuringly sober so that they know that they are free to be high. You are going to be responsible for them and keep track of reality for them. This lets the trippers relax, enjoy the experience, and not have to keep control of whatever it is that they think that they need to be in control of. Hang out with them if you like, take them for a walk. Be the person who makes the perfect snack appear at just the right moment. It can be a lot of fun to use your sobriety like a magician, facilitating the wonder of first time trippers.

When taking trippers out into public spaces, you

are the chaperone. You get to drive the car, buy the tickets, and make sure that no one lags too far behind. Depending on dosage and experience levels, managing trippers can be like herding cats. While this is no problem inside someone's home, it can be rather challenging when trying to get a handful of people through any point requiring tickets. Don't expect them to act like normal adults, expect them to act like preschoolers. That way you won't be taken off guard when one of them becomes hyper-fixated on something and loses track of what's going on.

When being Ground Control for a solo trip, your job is to stay out of the way, quiet and unseen unless needed. The solo tripper needs you to be there just in case the doorbell rings or anxiety rears its head. Don't fall asleep until they are mostly down. This could mean a late night for you as psychedelics have a stimulating effect. You should be able to gauge when it is appropriate to leave the trippers on their own. Let them know that they can wake you up if they need anything. Don't get in any way incapacitated yourself. Have fun, but bring a book. You might be bored, so have something to do that won't disrupt their experience or be difficult to interrupt.

Regardless of the setting, be available and

approachable, even if you aren't always interacting with the trippers. They should never feel
like they are interrupting or bugging you if they
need help with something. If they do come to
you for support, exude the "it's all good" vibe,
let them know that you're prepared to be the
responsible one, no matter what.

Ground Control is vital for "designated driv-
er/sober perspective" activities. I've seen very
experienced trippers get so high that crossing
the street became a challenging activity. Beyond
those types of situations, it is also important to
have Ground Control for the rare times when
a tripper becomes anxious. Anxiety can spiral
out of control and create a bad trip. Even trips
where a bad thing happens can be saved if the
bad thing can be resolved without excessive anxiety. A little bit of anxiety that is then managed
can be a useful part of an experience, but do not
allow anxiety to overwhelm the tripper.

How can you tell the difference? Most anxiety
in a trip is going to be useful, and helping a tripper explore that anxiety through conversations
can be very rewarding. Anxiety that needs to be
leaned into and processed is usually intellectual
and complex. Ask them questions about what it
means and how it could be resolved. Their brains
are very plastic and will make intuitive leaps.

This type of anxiety is more likely to lead to an epiphany than a bad trip if the tripper is willing to process it.

On the other hand, a hyper-fixation might be expressed as a sense of dread or ugly visuals. This type of anxiety is difficult to confront head on. Go back to the basics of Set, Setting, and Substance and change something. You may have to change their setting to make their set more flexible. Move to another room, find a safer space, embark on an adventure through the magical land of Not Where They Were. Something as small as getting someone to stand up can have an effect. Changing the setting can facilitate changing the set (the tripper's mindset) by drawing the tripper's attention to something else which gives them a path out of the anxiety spiral. Keep talking while changing the setting to enhance the effect of changing their sensory inputs. Move to a different room and talk about what is going on there. Go outside and look at something beautiful. Bring them to someone in a good mood. Be sure to let them know that this will pass and that others have had this experience before them. This could put the tripper into a place where they are able and willing to process whatever their mind needs to process.

But if the tripper's anxiety is becoming destructive and is resistant to the changes in the set and setting, you may have to change the substance. This should be considered a last resort and approached with caution. To do this, administer a substance that will induce relaxation. If you have access to valium, it is the best substance for reducing anxiety, but any benzodiazepine will work. Beta blockers can also be used to reduce anxiety. Again, sedatives should be used only as a last resort. In all my extensive experiences with psychedelics, I have only come across a few instances where administering a sedative was the best solution. In each of those situations, the tripper was both not in the right set to be tripping in the first place, and had consumed an excessive amount of psychedelics.

Whatever tactic is used, be sure to sit with the crisis until it passes. Do not leave the tripper alone. Guide the conversation with positive ideas and draw their attention to beauty. En-courage them to trust themselves and not hide from their own awareness. While it can be very unpleasant to experience anxiety during a trip, it can also be very enlightening. Sometimes we have to take the path through darkness to learn something important about ourselves. As Ground Control, it can be very rewarding to support someone as they make that journey and discover new ways to become their best self.

Getting the tripper to explain what is happening in their mind helps to dispel irrational thoughts as well as encourage their insights to surface. Ask leading questions like, "How does that make you feel?" and "What does that mean to you?" and try to really understand their answers. Feeling heard is incredibly comforting and can ease negative emotions.

Ultimately, being Ground Control is the psychedelic equivalent of being the designated driver. It might be boring, it might be exciting, but it is definitely a great way to keep your friends safe as they have a wild time.

ACKNOWLEDGEMENTS

Thank you to my fellow Leriati for your companionship and wisdom. Thank you to my readers, Vinski, Hurwood, Hastings. Thank you to Mr. Windsor for encouraging me to write this and for all his efforts in helping me get it across the finish line.

RESOURCES

Books

Essential Substances, by Richard Rudgley (prehistoric use of drugs)

From Chocolate to Morphine, by Andrew Weil & Winifred Rosen (textbook on recreational drugs)

How to Change Your Mind, by Michael Pollan (understanding modern psychedelic use)

PIHKAL: A Chemical Love Story, by Alexander & Ann Shulgin (notes from inventors & explorers of psychedelics)

Fantastic Fungi: How Mushrooms Can Heal, Shift Consciousness & Save the Planet, Edited by Paul Stamets

Web Resources

Erowid.org - documenting the complex relationship between humans and psychoactives

Psychonaut Wiki - a community-driven online encyclopedia that aims to document the emerging field of psychonautics in a comprehensive, scientifically grounded manner

Tripsit - harm reduction in the use of psychoactive substances.

Music to Trip To

John Hopkins YouTube and Spotify playlists

https://www.youtube.com/watch?v=JYsn76AL-frw

https://open.spotify.com/playlist/6eD2isTqIlg-moywT4ie3LR

Bands I like to trip to:

Air

Beats Antique

Bonobo

Brian Jonestown Massacre

Depeche Mode

Flaming lips (post Yoshimi)

Jamiroquai

Lamb

Mazzy Star

Morphine

The Orb

Phish

Portishead

Thievery Corporation

The Verve

William Orbit

About the Author

A. Zimmerman is a mother, artist, and adventurer, a Maker of Things, and a Dreamer of Dreams.